MONET

DISCOVERING ART

The Life, Times and Work of the World's Greatest Artists

MONET

K. E. SULLIVAN

BROCKHAMPTON PRESS

For Nana, who would have loved it

The author would like to acknowledge John House's *Nature into Art*
and Richard Kendall's *Monet by Himself*, both of which offered insight and inspiration.
Thanks also to Carey Wells for leading me out of the mire;
I couldn't have done it without you.

First published in Great Britain by Brockhampton Press,
an imprint of The Caxton Publishing Group,
20 Bloomsbury Street, London WC1B 3JH

Reprinted 2004

ISBN 1 84186 097 2

Produced by Flame Tree Publishing,
The Long House, Antrobus Road, Chiswick, London W4 5HY
for Brockhampton Press
A Wells/McCreeth/Sullivan Production

Printed and bound by Oriental Press, Dubai

CONTENTS

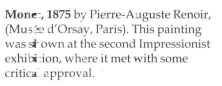

Monet, 1875 by Pierre-Auguste Renoir, (Musée d'Orsay, Paris). This painting was shown at the second Impressionist exhibition, where it met with some critical approval.

CHRONOLOGY

1840	Claude Oscar Monet born in Paris.
1845	Monet moves with his parents and family to Le Havre.
1856	Monet is introduced to outdoor painting by Boudin.
1861-2	Military service; visits Algiers.
1862	Enters the studio of Charles Gleyre, where he meets Bazille, Renoir and Sisley.
1865	Two paintings accepted at the Salon.
1867	Monet's first son, Jean, is born.
1869	Lives at Bougival; works with Renoir and Bazille.
1870	Marries his mistress Camille Doncieux.
1871	Paints in Holland; moves to Argenteuil, which remains his home for seven years.
1874	First exhibition of *Société Anonyme des peintures, etc.*; Monet's *Impression, Sunrise*, leads to the name Impressionism.
1876	Paints Decorations for businessman Hoschedé.
1878	Birth of Monet's second son, Michel; moves to Paris from Argenteuil, and then on to Vétheuil with the Hoschedé family.
1879	Camille Doncieux Monet dies.
1881	Moves to Poissy with Alice Hoschedé and her children.
1883	Paints at Etretat; moves from Poissy to Giverny.
1888	Refuses the Legion of Honour.
1889	Major retrospective exhibition of his work in the gallery of Georges Petit; paints at Antibes.
1890	Buys home at Giverny.
1892	Marries Alice Hoschedé; paints Rouen Cathedral.
1895	Paints in Norway.
1899	First series of paintings of his water garden at Giverny.
1900-1	Paints in London.
1908	Paints in Venice.
1911	Death of Alice Hoschedé Monet.
1912	Eyesight failing; cataracts determined to be the cause.
1914	Builds a new studio in his garden at Giverny; begins Water Lily Decorations.
1922	Water Lily Decorations donated to France; installed at the Orangerie in Paris.
1926	Dies at Giverny.

The Garden Path at Giverny, 1902
(Private Collection). The garden path
leads up to the house, lined with
nasturtiums and bound by trellises. The
expanse of colour and light was ever-
changing, daily and seasonally, when
different plants were encouraged to
flower.

CHAPTER 1

First Impressions

'I want to paint the air in which the bridge, the house and the boat are to be found – the beauty of the air around them, and that is nothing less than the impossible.'

Monet

The most powerful exponent of the French Impressionists, Claude Oscar Monet, was born in 1840, the son of an affluent Parisian grocer. He was born by the Seine, the river which flows through the heart of Paris and into eastern France. For the rest of his life he would make his home by its banks, travelling a great deal, but always returning to its shimmering familiarity. Water was an obsession for Monet; from his earliest days he would paint it, struggle to capture its light, reflections and colour. The waters of the Seine ran through his soul as surely as they would weave their way through his work.

Monet's family was not artistic, but Monet's skills were recognized, and to a certain extent encouraged. He was educated at La Meilleraye, a good school in Le Havre, where his family had moved when he was a child, and, slightly bored and perhaps creatively stifled, Monet became notorious for the irreverent caricatures he made of his classmates, his teachers, and then his neighbours. As he grew older his talent was celebrated locally and an exhibition of his caricatures eventually appeared, sponsored by a Le Havre picture dealer.

When Monet was eighteen he met Eugène Boudin, and this was reputedly the determining factor in his decision to become a painter. Boudin was a local landscape painter, but he had already achieved some recognition among his peers; in particular, Constant Troyon, Thomas Couture and Jean François Millet, each of whom painted in a different style but all of whom had obtained considerable contemporary success.

Boudin himself painted out of doors, documenting with splendid precision and originality the movement of water, air, clouds, trees; in fact, everything that a moment in nature presented. Boudin was extraordinarily influential in Monet's life, and he has been accorded the honour of being the Impressionists' first real inspiration. Boudin admired the work of Monet, and he recognized his gift for colour. Monet wrote later:

> One day Boudin said to me, '... appreciate the sea, the light, the blue sky.' I took his advice and together we went on long outings during which I painted constantly from nature. This was how I came to understand nature and learned to love it passionately.

Monet continued his relationship with Boudin for some time, sharing revelations and disappointments in his early career and seeking advice from the older painter on a regular basis. It was Boudin who offered him the necessary introductions in Paris, one of whom was Constant Troyon, who perceived the charm with which the young artist was able to portray a scene, but who also recognized the compositional flaws and the need for some serious study. Troyon was one of the Barbizon school of painters who worked on the edge of the Forest

of Fontainebleau, led by Theodore Rousseau; Monet himself would one day work there and it is likely that the Barbizon painters set the stage for the Impressionist movement, which would follow several years later.

Monet wrote to Boudin in 1859, quoting Troyon as saying, '... learn to draw: that's where most of you are falling down today ... draw with all your might; you can never learn too much. However, don't neglect painting, go to the country from time to time and make studies and above all develop them ...'

On the strength of Troyon's criticism, Monet's father reluctantly agreed to finance a two-month period of learning in Paris. Monet's mother had died in 1857 and with her most of the familial encouragement he had ever received. His father firmly believed that Monet belonged in the family business and was reluctant to finance a venture that he considered somewhat foppish, but he allowed Monet to go to Paris, thinking perhaps that the idea would soon lose its appeal. Once there Monet would be free to visit the Louvre, study

Still-life with Bottles, 1859 (Private Collection). In the early days of his aborted academic education, Monet painted anything which would earn him enough to live on. His composition was never good, but his flair for colour and light was exemplary even in these immature works.

from the masters, and, most importantly, apply to attend the famous Ecole des Beaux-Arts.

Academic training was rigidly defined in nineteenth-century France; a painter must not only excel among his peers at the Ecole, where it was expected that any serious artist would study, but he must also spend time at an academy of one of the recognized and accepted academic tutors.

Claude Monet was absolutely determined to be a painter. He was serious, but he was also single-minded and it is unlikely that he took any notice of what was considered acceptable and necessary for technical and traditional definitions of success. He wasn't interested in training, he wanted to learn first hand; most importantly, he just wanted to *paint*. He associated himself with painters on the fringe of the establishment; he refused to attend the Ecole des Beaux-Arts. Monet's father was a patient man, but his son was a free spirit, and a more academic approach was clearly necessary to procure a career in art. The financial expenditure necessary to allow Monet to philander in Paris was more than his father was willing to provide, and Monet's allowance was cut off.

In order to re-establish some financial support, Monet enrolled in the Académie Suisse, a small private art school where he met Camille Pissarro. Monet's father failed to be impressed, and despite his good intentions, Monet simply wasn't inspired by the strictures of training. He left shortly after, but remained friends with Pissarro, an important precursor to the Impressionist movement.

It is a tribute to his tenacity that Monet eventually became a financial success. His self-proclaimed integrity prevented him from studying something with which he did not agree, and his wanderlust and spontaneity ensured that he did not spend any extended period of time in one place. Certainly a skilled and imaginative painter, he lacked academic training and he felt little need to acquire it. He liked to paint with his colleagues, to work out of doors. He disliked from the very beginning the confines of the studio and the rigid approach accepted by his contemporaries. But nature provided little in the way of regular sustenance and lodgings, not to mention paint and canvas, and Monet was forced to paint anything that would attract some financial support. For many years he painted still-lifes, portraits and studies, but his heart remained in the outdoors, and he publicly denounced much of the art that he was forced to undertake.

Landscape painting was considered the poor relation of the more established categories of painting, but he would relentlessly pursue it, in defiance, perhaps, of everything that was believed to be important about art in those days.

Monet's lust for painting was firmly checked by two years in military service in Northern Africa. He returned, at the age of twenty-two, weakened by typhoid fever, but more determined than ever to

Spring Flowers, 1864 (Cleveland Museum of Art). Monet had always been fascinated with flowers, calling his garden and his painting his only true interests in life. Wherever he was able to set down roots he created an eye-catching garden which he could paint, he said, when it rained.

Déjeuner sur l'Herbe (Luncheon on the Grass), 1865-6 (Pushkin Museum, Moscow). Inspired by Manet's notorious painting of the same name, Monet painted this work out of doors, with a patient Camille Doncieux and Frédéric Bazille acting as models. The influence of Courbet is evident in the painting, and Monet was never happy with it.

succeed. While convalescing at Le Havre, he met the Dutch painter Johan Barthold Jongkind, a landscape artist whose evocative and fresh style had been admired by Monet and Boudin for many years. Monet was enormously inspired by Jongkind and he returned to painting with a new enthusiasm and vision; he later wrote that Jongkind had completed the 'education of my eye', and indeed the older artist played an important role in the development of the technique which would eventually characterize Impressionism, with exquisite studies of the effects of air and atmosphere, painted in the *plein air*.

Again, lack of money put paid to Monet's grandiose plans; models and paint were expensive and living even more so. Monet's family had always been comfortable, and although his father's business had occasionally hit upon hard times, they had never done without, spending long vacations at popular resorts, and entire summers with his Aunt Sophie at Saint Adresse, a coastal town in Normandy. The situation was frustrating for Monet, who loved good food and drink, and the company of women and like-minded colleagues. He wanted to get on with things, to experience the sparkling world around him.

Paris was a fascinating and vibrant place in the 1850s and 1860s; café society was at its height and the city had become a mecca for bright, impressive young men and women. Industrialization had freed society from drudgery and nowhere was it more obvious than in the bubbling, stimulating streets of Paris. Food, chatter, colour and light were plentiful; even those with little money could breathe in the atmosphere, experience the energy.

But poverty was and would become an ever-growing burden to Monet. He grudgingly agreed to take up academic study again, in order to receive some financial support from his father, but he lasted only a few weeks. He entered the studio of Charles Gleyre because he was a respected academic master, and because he didn't expect too much from his students; it was understood that Gleyre encouraged individuality, and Monet was in favour of that. But in principle, Monet despised the academic tradition, and he felt he had nothing to learn from the Swiss-born Gleyre. He said that Gleyre was 'of no help to his pupils ... we were well rid of it', and he returned to painting out of doors, this time with the new friends he had made at the studio Gleyre.

Pierre-Auguste Renoir, Alfred Sisley and Frédéric Bazille were drawn to the studio of Charles Gleyre for much the same reasons as Monet; Gleyre had a reputation for relaxed principles and teaching methods, and he was also a less expensive option for what was, for the most part, an impoverished group of artists. Bazille and Sisley had some money behind them – in particular, Bazille would, until his untimely death in the Franco-Prussian War, support both Renoir and Monet when they had trouble eking out a living from their work. Renoir came from working-class parents who were unable to contribute in any way to their son's education, and Monet was frequently out of favour with his, so that both were required to live meagrely, and often on the generosity of their friends. The four men became firm friends, their inspired ideology drawing the first breath of the movement that would become Impressionism.

His colleagues were in general more disciplined and perhaps more bohemian than Monet, but they delighted in their new companion. Renoir described Monet as a 'dandy' to his son Jean who wrote, in his book, *Renoir on Renoir*:

He didn't have a sou, but he wore shirts with lace cuffs. To one student who was making up to him, a pretty but vulgar girl, he replied: 'I'm sorry but I only sleep with duchesses or maids. Anything in between I find revolting. The ideal would be a duchess's maid.'

The men painted together at the Forest of Fontainebleau, Monet having abandoned his formal training and, again, his allowance in favour of working in the fresh air. Many chance meetings throughout this period led to the development of his technique, and the painters all sought inspiration from each other. For all his self-confidence and blustering enthusiasm, however, Monet was aware that the only path to financial success in the 1860s lay through the Salon, the prestigious annual exhibition held at the Louvre in Paris at which the very best painters, in the opinion of the rather staid and official jury, had their work represented. Critics and potential patrons frequented the Salon and a successful exhibition might guarantee a certain number of lucrative commissions for an artist. The selection of paintings at the Salon reflected very much the academic traditions and the artistic tastes of the establishment. There was very little scope for creative ventures and the same styles were represented over and over again.

Astonishingly Monet's first submissions were accepted: *Cape La Hève at Ebb Tide* and *The Mouth of the Seine at Honfleur* in 1865, and *Camille* and a further seascape in 1866. Flushed with his early success, he began to undertake more challenging paintings, all of which were rejected. Poverty rankled with Monet, and his copious correspondence with his friends over the next decades echoed his concern about making a living. He was briefly supported by his generous Aunt Sophie – particularly when he had achieved a modicum of critical attention, which impressed her – and Bazille repeatedly offered help in the form of food, housing and financial aid, but Monet was determined to paint for a living and he found his lack of success more than daunting.

He experimented with various styles, incorporating especially the techniques of Courbet, Jongkind, Millet and his friend Renoir. Courbet in particular had designs on the young artist's work, and because he was in the position to offer him some financial support, Courbet indulged himself by pressing his opinions on the often irate Monet, who retaliated by undertaking some of his suggestions, and then abandoning Courbet altogether.

Edouard Manet also influenced the group of young artists; very much the *enfant terrible* of the art scene, he was both denounced and admired for his revolutionary use of paint and his natural, contemporary subjects. Manet had found a champion in the poet Baudelaire, and Monet and his friends were new recruits to his growing ideology. It was Manet who first put into words what the Impressionists stood for, even if it was Monet's work which would eventually give it a name.

Manet's infamous *Déjeuner sur l'Herbe* was the inspiration for Monet's own painting of the same name. Manet's painting set a properly composed luncheon in a clearing in the woods. Its main proponents, however, were two city gentlemen accompanied by two very nude young ladies. There was no attempt to attribute their nudity to any classical source, or to give it a meaning, and it was labelled pornographic. Manet's style was reckless, with a cheerful

The Terrace at St Adresse, 1866 (Metropolitan Museum of Art, New York). Monet's choice of colour reflects his earlier realistic work, but he has begun to experiment with the rendition of light; it glints from the flags, the sea, his subject's dress, and the central parasol, a compelling and quite revolutionary painting for that time.

use of paint that shamelessly disregarded the dogma of the contemporary schools of art.

Not surprisingly, the lively Monet was impressed by Manet's rebelliousness, but he was not in a position to undertake anything so flagrantly different. He needed a Salon success, so he caught on to the coat-tails of Manet and attempted his own, very large version of the same painting – with, interestingly, the young ladies fully clothed. An attempt to give, in his own words, 'a scene of everyday bourgeois recreation the scale and status of a history painting', Monet's *Déjeuner sur l'Herbe* was intended to be painted in the spirit of Manet, but actually out of doors. An ambitious project, it threw Monet into a flurry of excitement, and he painted the vast canvas in Paris, helped financially by Courbet. The latter regularly offered advice, which greatly irritated Monet, but swallowing his integrity he accepted it and made changes to his great work – to the extent that he no longer liked it and left the canvas rolled up for many years.

Monet had worked tirelessly on the painting, travelling daily to the forest of Fontainebleau with his lover Camille Doncieux and his friend Bazille, who sat hour after hour as the subjects for the painting. However, just weeks before the selection for 1865 Salon exhibition was made, he realized that he would not finish it in time, and he put the painting to one side. Monet's pre-Impressionist naturalism is evident in the work, as is his growing interest in light – the sunlight on the foliage, the glimmer of light through the trees with their shadows and reflective foliage. The painting was a studio composition worked from studies, but he has captured the effect of sunlight in a manner that Manet, whose own painting was the product of studio lighting, was unable. The painting is, however, a tribute to his alliance with Manet.

Despite Monet's unashamed admiration for the painter, Manet was suspicious of the young artist, not only because of the growing similarity of their work, but also because of their virtually identical names. It was a long time before Manet would trust the younger painter, seeming to suspect, somehow, that Monet had adopted his name in order to trick the public.

It was partly Manet's one-man show in the gallery of the famous dealer Martinet which inspired Monet, Sisley and eventually Renoir to leave the the studio of Gleyre, in order to paint without supervision. The young artists were restless with the academic approach to art that was required by students of the Ecole, and indeed any of the academic masters. Monet's fascination with the outdoors was becoming an obsession and he longed to find the means by which he could capture the atmosphere, the very air around him. But necessity required a different course.

He painted anything that he thought might sell, even attempting to make money as a cartoonist, and when success continued to elude him, he suffered from long periods of depression and disenchantment. But he worked relentlessly at his art, and struggled to attract buyers and patrons.

Monet's personal affairs were also growing more complicated. His lover, a nineteen-year-old girl of humble origins, was Camille Doncieux, the *Camille*, of his first Salon acceptance. She had been his model since the time they met, in about 1865, and he was passionately in love with her. Monet was a gourmand when it came to women and he found Camille a veritable feast. With dark hair and serious eyes, she was an attractive and clearly intelligent woman. Monet's family were horrified by her background, and in order to curry favour he was forced to pretend they did not live together, although it was evident from his paintings at the time that she was very much a part of his life.

Camille, 1866 (Bremen Kunsthalle). Allegedly painted in only a few days, when *Déjeuner sur l'Herbe* was not completed in time for Salon acceptance, this work is a splendid tribute to Monet's talents. The critics swooned at his handling of the silk of Camille's dress. In the magazine *La Lune,* they wrote, 'Bravo Monet!'

Until her death, Camille Doncieux was Monet's one and only model and she sat for him in almost every conceivable setting, patiently allowing him to create around her. She was a warm, self-possessed woman, expecting nothing, but enjoying, like Monet, the good things when they were able to afford them.

In 1867, Camille gave birth to their first son, Jean, and the three-some took up residence together, adding to his financial burden. Monet was disinherited once more by his family, and that year he failed again to get any official support. He felt persecuted by poverty, and denied of his rightful position; he had no qualms about plaguing

Stormy Sea at Etretat, 1868 (Musée d'Orsay, Paris). Just prior to the Franco-Prussian War, Monet spent a great deal of time painting along the northern coast of France. Etretat captured his imagination and he returned to paint here many times over the next decades.

his friends with requests for money, becoming unjustifiably angered when they were refused. He berated his friend Bazille for his lack of support:

I really don't know what to say to you, you've shown such pig-headedness in not replying ... Once again I had to borrow and received snubs from people I don't know ... I'm going through the most terrible torments, I had to come back here [Sainte-Adresse] not to upset the family and also because I didn't have enough money to stay in Paris while Camille was in labour. She has given birth to a

big and beautiful boy and despite everything I feel that I love him, and it pains me to think of his mother having nothing to eat.

The following year was more promising. At Etretat, a coastal town in Normandy, renowned for its magnificent cliffs, to which he would return many times over the years, Monet felt a swell of the old enthusiasm. A new patron had materialized and, delighting in the seascape and free of financial worries, Monet was able to get on with his work. He wrote to Bazille about his new contentment:

I'm very happy, very delighted ... for I am surrounded here by all that I love. I spend my time out of doors ... and naturally I'm working all the time, and I think this year I'm going to do some serious things. And then in the evening, dear fellow, I come home to my little cottage to find a good fire and a dear little family ... Dear friend, it's a delight to watch this person grow, and I'm glad to have him to be sure ...

The next summer, in 1869, Renoir and Monet painted together at La Grenouillère, an outdoor bathing spot on the Seine, just outside of Paris. Their work there set the stage for what would become one of the most popular schools of art in the world. With easels almost touching, the two young artists painted the merry scenes in front of them with a gloriously unrestrained palette. Their paintings rippled with life, light and laughter, patches of diverse colour working to intimate the essence of a scene rather than its reality. The painters struggled to find money for paint and food, but they were heady days filled with the rich sense of accomplishment. Their paintings were unstructured, and there is some evidence that the artists themselves considered them sketches for later, grander works, but their sparkle and spontaneity was immediately engaging, and Renoir and Monet soon realized that they had achieved a brilliance that was missing from much of their earlier work.

Monet wrote to Bazille in September 1869: 'I do have a dream, a tableau of the bathing place of La Grenouillère, for which I've done some bad *pochades* [sketches], but it is a dream. Renoir, who has just spent a couple of months here, also wants to paint this subject.' It is interesting to note that it was these same 'bad sketches' which would become some of the greatest examples of Impressionist art ever painted.

Monet's good friend Renoir was happier to live and paint in poverty. Often a cheerful optimist, he wrote, 'We don't eat every day. Yet I am happy in spite of it, because, as far as painting is concerned, Monet is good company. I do almost nothing because I haven't much paint.' Monet, with a family to support, was bitter about their plight: 'Here I am at a halt, from lack of paints. Only I this year will have done

Women in a Garden, 1866-7 (Musée d'Orsay, Paris). Painted just after *Déjeuner sur l'Herbe,* this painting was another challenging but largely unsuccessful experiment. His use of light is exemplary, but the figures are unrealistic. His lover, Camille Doncieux, is seated at the front.

nothing. This makes me rage against everybody. I'm jealous, mean, I'm going mad. If I could work, everything would go all right.'

These pre-Impressionist paintings had the spontaneity of a photograph, but the visionary impact of something much more subtle. The artists didn't seek realism, recreating instead the effect of a brief period of time with daubs of colour and texture that represent clearly the light and atmosphere of that moment. Accents of colour replaced drawing, and touches of paint took the place of any kind of formal structure. Critics of the day considered these paintings grossly unfinished.

La Grenouillère was an important painting for Monet; in it he experiments with the kind of composition that would become characteristic of his work for years to come. Dr John House, in *Nature into Art*, wrote:

> *La Grenouillère of 1869 introduces a type of composition which dominated Monet's work for the next decade and remained important throughout his life. A succession of horizontal planes face the spectator; forms reflected in water link foreground and distance, unifying the surface of the picture without recourse to traditional types of spatial recession; by changes of scale and emphasis, the reflected forms suggest a progression across the stretches of water ...*

Monet's style was developing quite differently from that of his colleagues, but they were united in their belief that art must be less realistic, more representative. Their collective genius was later classed 'eye disease', but their extraordinary perception was taking root in the varying styles of each painter.

In 1870, the Franco-Prussian War brought to a halt the plans of this group of young, perceptive artists. Renoir served active duty in Algiers, where he nearly died, and Bazille was killed, his promising career cut tragically short. Monet, newly married to Camille, and fearing conscription, fled to London with his wife, where they remained for two years. Monet was badly affected by the death of his friend Bazille, who had been confidant, mentor, saviour on more than one occasion, and godfather to his son Jean. For some time after his death, Monet kept to himself, continuing to work but clearly missing his friend enormously.

The years in London were good to Monet and Camille, and they spent a great deal of time in the company of, and often supported by, Pissarro, who had some money behind him and was intrigued by the decidedly strong-willed Monet. They left England following the war, travelling through Holland where Monet stopped to paint several times, in particular at the port of Zaandam, to which he would return again in the future. They settled eventually at Argenteuil, a leafy town on the Seine, north-east of Paris, into which the café society of Paris

spilled on weekends. Monet's father had died and left his son some money; with this, and Camille's dowry, they were able to rent a comfortable home, and live stylishly for several years.

Argenteuil offered new hope for Monet and his family, and they would remain there for nearly eight years. It was a period that represented the realization of Impressionism, the movement that would eventually buy Monet his place in history.

Zuiderkerk, Amsterdam, 1872 (Philadelphia Museum of Art). Monet visited Amsterdam immediately following his exile in London during the war against Prussia. The influence of Pissarro is evident in his choice of colours, and in the ever-decreasing size of the brushstrokes.

CHAPTER 2

Upturns and Upset

'I am absolutely sickened with and demoralized by this life I've been leading for so long. When you reach my age, there is nothing more to look forward to. Unhappy we are, unhappy we will continue to be.'

Monet

Overleaf:
Impression, Sunrise, 1872 (Musée Marmottan, Paris). Monet struck upon the name for this painting on impulse, just before the first Impressionist exhibition opened. It was this painting which inspired the name Impressionism.

The years following the Franco-Prussian War were fairly prosperous years for Monet, who was now in his mid-thirties and old enough to appreciate his new-found wealth. The art dealer Paul Durand-Ruel, with whom Monet would form a lifelong relationship, was purchasing his work regularly, and Monet could afford to rent good-sized homes and surround them with exquisite scenery. The first of his homes at Argenteuil is documented in *Monet's House at Argenteuil* (1873), and they moved here in 1871 when Jean was only four. Monet once said that his two great loves in life were painting and gardens, and at Argenteuil he indulged these loves, creating an extraordinary garden, filled with luxurious, brilliantly coloured displays of flowers and trees, and painting his family and friends amongst their splendour. He felt that nature was a sanctuary from life – salve for the spirit – and he was increasingly disenchanted with the unloveliness of contemporary architecture and commercial developments. His garden became the centre of his world, and from that time at Argenteuil, he ensured that every home in which he lived had one.

The Monet family lived well at Argenteuil; the canvases painted here show an elegant and cultivated lifestyle – china teacups, maids, lovely frocks and a splendid garden that was created at some expense and maintained by a gardener. There are glimpses of well-polished furniture and shining chandeliers, all emblems of a certain prosperity. It was one to which Monet was accustomed, and which Camille grew to love.

Monet's painting at Argenteuil became remarkably polished; he had found landscape painting, although critically frowned upon, a perfect vehicle for his talents and throughout this period he produced a stunning variety of work. Monet painted the streets of Argenteuil, his own family and gardens and most importantly the effects of light on the Seine. He converted a small boat into a studio in order to travel along the river, to paint the light and atmospheric conditions that so fascinated him. Richard Kendall, in *Monet by Himself*, wrote:

> *Along the banks of the Seine the curious juxtapositions of modern suburban life were much in evidence, ornate weekend villas contrasting with vast steel bridges and delicate pleasure craft with distant factory chimneys. Monet's art flourished among these contradictions, at times celebrating the stark modernity of* The Railway Bridge at Argenteuil *and at others recording the simple play of light in* Poplars, near Argenteuil. *While Monet chose to turn his back on much of the industrial landscape at Argenteuil, his studies of the 1870s show a marked preference for sites where 'nature' has been modified by the intervention of human society.*

Monet's work came to define much of what the Impressionist movement would become; his pure colours were layered with tiny brushstrokes, filling in the vision of a moment in nature with dancing touches of broken colour. He painted quickly, swift eager brushstrokes betraying his enthusiasm, and capturing the subtle effects of the changing light. He publicly scorned studio painting, moving along the Seine in a languid manner, probing the hues and illumination that changed with every passing moment.

He painted huge numbers of canvases over the years at Argenteuil; the changing seasons, paths, meadows, trees, parks and his family were favourite subjects, and he painted the railway bridge at Argenteuil in almost every conceivable light, delighting in the contrast of the new and the old.

The Artist's Garden at Argenteuil, 1872 (Chicago Art Institute). Four-year-old Jean Monet appears in the foreground of this lustrous portrayal of the garden at Monet's first home at Argenteuil. The blue-and-white ceramic pots were purchases in Holland, following the Franco-Prussian War, and he moved them from home to home.

Jean on a Wheeled Horse, 1872 (Private Collection). Jean, Monet's eldest son, was the subject of much of Monet's earlier work, before he decided to concentrate almost exclusively on landscapes.

Argenteuil was in easy reach of Paris by train, via the Gare Saint-Lazare, a central railway station, and Monet was visited often by friends and colleagues who came to paint the startlingly beautiful stretch of countryside. Many of the painters who came to be associated with the budding Impressionist movement met here, including Renoir, Sisley, Caillebotte and Manet, a group often called the Batignolles group, who had spent considerable time together in the early 1870s at Café Gúerbois, in the Batignolles region of Paris, where many artists and writers lived and worked. From the late 1860s, Edouard Manet was the centre of evening gatherings in the local Café Gúerbois, where animated discussions on modern art and literature took place, and he was joined by numerous of the other men and women who would become the Impressionists.

The Impressionist fascination with modern-life theme often

focused on the contemporary urban world of leisure and entertainment and Paris was the hub of their world. Monet was friendly with various controversial writers, including Zola and Astruc, and like many of his contemporaries, he enjoyed battling out the emerging doctrines of their age. But he did find the Parisian intelligentsia somewhat daunting company, and a distraction from the vision he had for his work. In 1868 he wrote to Bazille commenting on his disillusionment:

> One is too taken up with all that one sees and hears in Paris, however strong one is, and what I do here will at least have the merit of being unlike anyone else, at least I believe so, because it will simply be the expression of what I, and only I, have felt. The further I get, the more I regret how little I know, that's what hinders me the most ... It's strange ... I don't think I will spend much time in Paris now, a month at the very most, each year ...

Jean on a Wheeled Horse, 1872 (detail) (Private Collection). Monet's figures were never as accomplished as his landscapes but he shared a close relationship with his family and continued to paint them in luxuriant settings over the years.

The aims of the group were, however, shared with regard to their work. Each was becoming dissatisfied with the process by which paintings were chosen for exhibition at the Salon, and the work of these painters was increasingly rejected. They sought an answer to the dilemma of the outdated jury system, and had begun to consider the idea of yet another alternative exhibition. The war had firmly quashed any earlier plans for such an exhibition, but by 1874 the time seemed ripe to plan an independent exhibition aimed at those artists who painted what they themselves described as 'nature and life in their larger realities'.

A large selection of artists were included in the exhibition, partly because the show was to be funded by the contributors themselves, and partly because the organizers felt that artists who had already achieved some critical acclaim would lend authority to the venture. Renoir suggested the name for the group: *Société Anonyme des artistes, peintres, sculpteurs, graveurs, etc.* For a monthly subscription of five francs, artists could exhibit and sell their paintings. There would be no selection process, but there would be a committee presiding over the society, to ensure its smooth running. The first committee was an impressive list of names, including Pissarro, Degas, Sisley, Morisot, Guillaumin, Beliard, Renoir and Monet, among others. The exhibition was scheduled to open on 15 April, two weeks before the official Salon.

Impression, Sunrise, Monet's study of the port at Le Havre, painted in 1862, was only one of the works he exhibited, but it was this painting which caused the group of artists to be labelled Impressionists. Louis Leroy, writing for the satirical magazine *Le Charivari,* noted, 'Impression – too right! And I was just saying that if an impression has been made on me, something must be making it. What freedom and

Boulevard des Capucines, 1873
(Nelson-Atkins Museum of Art, Kansas City). The subjects of Monet's famous painting, which hung at the first Impressionist exhibition, were registered with tiny daubs and flicks of paint, presenting a hazy impression of a moment in Paris's heyday. The critics scorned it.

ease in the brushwork! Wallpaper in its embryonic state is more finished than this ...' The label was quickly adopted by others and within several months became an accepted term in the art world, defining the stylistic unity of the group. Monet was soon acknowledged as being a radical, influential and pre-eminent part of the group; in fact, Theodore Duret called him 'the Impressionist *par excellence*'.

Monet exhibited several paintings at the first Impressionist exhibition, including *Luncheon* which had been rejected for inclusion in the Salon exhibition of 1870, for being too bold, too unprofessional. While the exuberant handling of paint is often attributed to Manet's influence (Manet's own *Breakfast in the Studio*, shown at the Salon in 1969, may have been Monet's inspiration), it is a painting confirming Monet's mastery of colour and light. Interestingly, it is also a fascinating portrayal of Monet's lifestyle at this time, which was clearly prosperous.

Monet also included *Boulevard des Capucines*, one of his most thought-provoking works. The painting was undertaken from the window of the photographer Nadar's window, where the first Impressionist exhibition was held, and represents one of his most spectacular views of Paris. Richard Kendall comments on the significance of the work: 'Monet drew attention to the paradoxical relationship between art and observed reality, while at the same time making new claims for the immediacy and topicality of his art.'

Unfortunately, the critics in attendance failed to reach the same conclusions, labelling it crude and unfinished. In fact, Leroy, again in *Le Charivari*, blustered: 'Are you telling me that that is what I look like when I stroll along the Boulevard des Capucines ... Are you kidding?'

The first Impressionist exhibition was not a success in any way, although it did have the effect of bringing the group to the attention of the critics. Comparatively few members of the public attended the exhibition; the Salon for instance would attract anything up to 3500 visitors a day. The Impressionists' first exhibition drew about 175. At the best of times, the French were notorious for reacting with hostility to anything different; it happened each year at both the Salon and the Salon des Refusés, the other 'alternative' exhibition created by Napoleon III, in response to the protests of artists whose work had been refused by the Salon. But the animosity of the critics was unanticipated. While the term Impressionism became accepted among most critics, there was a faction who called the group 'The Intransigents', an expression which took its name from the radical political party that had attempted to take over the constitutional monarchy in Spain. The word came to mean anything that appeared to question the established order, and the Impressionists were seen by many to be an anarchic movement, threatening the existence of the established art tradition in France. The critic Leroy called their work:

The Luncheon, 1873 (Musée d'Orsay, Paris). Painted at Argenteuil, this work reflects Monet's increasingly affluent lifestyle. His splendid and well-tended garden is the backdrop for a very proper, and clearly civilized lunch. One expects the maid to appear at any moment.

... messy compositions, these thin washes, these mud-splashes against which the art lover has been rebelling for thirty years and which he has accepted only because constrained to do so ...

Many of the artists failed to sell anything at all, and the paintings were auctioned the following year, to disappointing prices and reception. Another exhibition was not planned, but, in 1866, when the Salon once again rejected the works of those we have come to know as the great proponents of the Impressionist movement, another exhibition was launched, this time in the gallery of the art dealer Paul Durand-Ruel, who had long been an admirer of the Impressionist

Gladiolas, 1873 (Detroit Institute of Art). Painted at Argenteuil, this work depicts Monet's magnificent garden. Camille holds a parasol.

work and one of the few dealers to have made substantial purchases.

The second exhibition was disastrous. The Impressionists had gained in some quarters a reputation for being seditious, and many of the critics made no attempt to disguise their antagonism. Albert Wolff, writing for the paper *Le Figaro*, said:

> Some people burst out laughing in front of these things – my heart is oppressed by them ... These self-styled artists who call themselves 'The Intransigents' or 'The Impressionists' take a canvas, some paint and brushes, throw some tones haphazardly on the canvas and then sign it. This is the way in which the lost souls of the Ville-Evrard [a notorious hospital for the mentally ill] pick up pebbles from the roadway, and believe that they have found diamonds.

There were, however, some grudging admirers of the style, and some, although they rejected the basic tenets of Impressionism, found their work food for thought. Henry James, writing for the *New York Tribune*, thought the group was:

> ... decidedly interesting. But the effect of it was to make me think better than ever of all the good old rules which decree that beauty is beauty and ugliness is ugliness, and warn us off from the sophisti-cations of satiety. The young contributors ... are partisans of unadorned reality and absolute foes to arrangement, embellishment, selection ... None of its members shows any signs of possessing

Europe Bridge, Gare Saint-Lazare, 1877 (Musée Marmottan, Paris). Monet was captivated by the railway bridge at the Saint-Lazare Station in Paris; the steam of the engines represented another atmospheric hue for him to capture on canvas.

first rate talent, and indeed the Impressionist doctrines strike me as incompatible, in an artist's mind, with the existence of first rate talent. To embrace them you must be provided with a plentiful absence of imagination.

Durand-Ruel had bought a large number of Monet's paintings previous to the exhibition – thirty in 1872 and thirty-four in 1873 – and the sum of 25,000 francs was paid for the final lot, which gave Monet a more than comfortable allowance upon which to live and support his family. After 1873, however, Durand-Ruel bought fewer and fewer Impressionist paintings. He'd over-extended himself supporting the group, and there seemed to be little interest in their work. He continued to show for the artists, but Monet, in particular, could no longer depend on receiving a decent income from the dealer. He was forced to look for other patrons, and to call upon the generosity of friends to support his lifestyle.

While he was able to continue to rent his home, Monet and Camille were forced to let go its staff, regularly selling personal items to make ends meet. Monet happily spent everything that came his way, putting nothing aside for leaner days. And when these arrived, as they are wont to do in a painter's life, Monet had to abandon his new lifestyle and struggle once more to put food on the table.

His painting throughout this period exhibited none of the stresses he was clearly feeling. His Impressionist technique had matured and he captured the world around him at Argenteuil with enthusiastic abandon. *The Basin at Argenteuil* (1872) and *Regatta at Argenteuil*, painted in the same year, represent the decreasing emphasis on reality in Monet's work; he sought more and more to capture the immediate impression, the essence of scene, rather than to document it with any accuracy. The result was a stunning new vocabulary of painting, where every syllable was represented with another dash of colour, a flamboyant and confident expression of what Monet actually felt.

He began a series of paintings in Paris – aggressive, harsh and strangely reverential portrayals of the *Gare Saint-Lazare*, which he travelled through each time he visited Paris from his home at Argenteuil. Monet seemed compelled by the tasteless modernity of the huge structure, and he gave it every glory he'd previously accorded only to nature. While he, like Renoir, hated the developments that arose with the Industrial Age, he was clearly fascinated by their reality, and their implications. The steam of the engines offered him a new perspective on shifting atmosphere, and the dirty air and gleaming metals and glass contrasted superbly under his brush.

An amusing story has emerged from his days spent painting at the Paris railway station. Once he had decided on this as his subject, he appeared there, dressed in his habitual finery, and said to the startled stationmaster, 'I am the painter, Claude Monet'. Not wishing to be considered a philistine, the manager allowed Monet countless courtesies, altering timetables when Monet insisted that a train remain in place while he finished a canvas, moving the trains to and fro according to the compositional requirements, and stopping and starting trains in order to produce the billows of steam. For days he returned to the station and imperiously gave orders to the awe-struck station staff, and then he left, a clutch of paintings under his arm, no one any the wiser about his identity or indeed significance.

In 1876, after a few lean years, Monet attracted the attention of the collector Ernest Hoschedé, a wealthy department store owner who was increasingly interested in the burgeoning art of the

Europe Bridge, Gare Saint-Lazare, 1877 (detail) (Musée Marmottan, Paris). Trains were stopped and started, schedules were re-arranged and trains moved back into position upon the whims of 'Claude Monet – painter'. A confused but clearly awe-struck stationmaster complied with all Monet's directions.

Impressionists. An extraordinary situation developed between the two families. Alice Hoschedé, Ernest's wife, and mother of their six children, formed a close relationship with Monet, and she and her family began to spend an inordinate amount of time with him. It has been suggested that her relations with Monet went beyond friendship, and that their growing dependence on one another jeopardized his own relationship with his wife. But there is also no doubt that Monet was still in love with Camille; he may possibly have compromised their relationship by an affair with Alice, but he returned always to Camille and clearly felt that the two families could become friends.

Life at Argenteuil was increasingly hard. In 1876, Monet wrote to Georges De Bellio, a doctor and patron of a number of the Impressionists: '...I can find no way out of it, the creditors are proving impossible to deal with and short of a sudden appearance on the scene of wealthy art patrons, we are going to be turned out of this dear little house ... I do not know what will become of us ...'

Ernest Hoschedé went bankrupt in 1877, which was a blow to Monet, who had come to rely on his financial support. It's likely that Hoschedé felt some responsibility for Monet and it was decided in 1878 that the two families would pool their resources and move in together in the village of Vétheuil, about forty miles west of Paris on the Seine. Camille Monet gave birth to their second son Michel, just previous to the move, but her health was failing and she seems to have been disheartened by the intimacy shared by her husband and Alice Hoschedé. Camille died in September 1879, after a long and painful illness, made worse by the commune-style existence they were living, and their growing poverty. Just prior to her death, Monet wrote again to Georges De Bellio, begging for some assistance, and voicing the terror he felt at his wife's condition:

For a long time I have been hoping for better days ahead, but alas, I believe the time has come for me to abandon all hope. My poor wife is in increasing pain ... One has to be at her bedside continually attending her smallest wish, in the hope of relieving her suffering, and the saddest thing is that we cannot always satisfy these immediate needs for lack of money. For a month now I have not been able to paint ... it is the sight of my wife's life in jeopardy that terrifies me, and it is unbearable ...

Monet cut himself off from most of his Paris set, and with Ernest Hoschedé spending more and more time away from the family home in Vétheuil, Monet and Alice were left to support and attend to eight children alone. Even more than that, he missed Camille deeply. She had been his constant companion for years and now she was dead, at

La Japonaise, 1876 (Boston Museum of Art). Camille donned a blonde wig for this painting, a tribute to the Japanese 'fever' which had swept the country since Japan was opened to the West in the mid-1800s. The painting was successful, sold at the second Impressionist exhibition, but it reflects more Monet's attempt to conform than it does his instinctive, more vibrant style.

La Promenade, 1875 (Private Collection). One of Monet's many interpretations of a walk on a summer's day the focus is, as usual, not the figures, but the stunning landscape.

only thirty-two years old. There was a rumour at the time that her illness was caused by a botched attempt at abortion, which creates an image of a desperate woman. Monet's despair was almost tangible. He wrote at the time:

> *I found myself at daybreak at the bedside of a dead woman who had been and always will be dear to me. My gaze was fixed on her tragic temples, and I caught myself observing the shades and nuances of colour Death brought to her countenance. Blues, yellows, greys, I don't know what. That is the state I was in ... Like a draught animal working at the millstone. Pity me ...*

He had few resources for painting, and no hope of an income without his livelihood. Throughout the long winter of 1880 he painted very little, and what he did manage to finish was melancholy, characterized by dull greys, blues – the morose associations of death. His paintings were empty of life, his seascapes free of birds and plantlife. He wrote letters to friends, begging for assistance, a shadow of the man he had been.

In 1880 Monet struck up again his association with Durand-Ruel. The early eighties found Monet dependent on most of his associates. Manet had made the move to Vétheuil possible by purchasing several of his canvases, but in 1883 he died, leaving another hole in Monet's life. Manet had become a close comrade and the younger man was the only Impressionist chosen to become a pallbearer at Manet's funeral. Monet also continued his friendship with Renoir, often painting at his side, but the two men had a growing rivalry about their art, arguing ceaselessly about the shortcomings of the other's work, which necessarily required that the time they spent painting together was limited. But Renoir was one of Monet's few remaining friends, and because he generally had less money than Monet, their relationship was never threatened by Monet's constant requests for aid.

Monet was becoming increasingly obsessed with painting out of doors, with capturing every aspect of light and atmosphere; while Renoir continued to paint landscapes, he found more pleasure in people and much of his work was characterized by the human form. Renoir's style differed from Monet's and their paintings, even those worked at the same moment, are immediately identifiable as their own.

Monet had met Pissarro in London following the outbreak of the Franco-Prussian War, and they kept in close contact through the years. But their friendship, like that of most of his friends, suffered throughout this period of depression, and Monet disagreed with Pissarro's vision for the Impressionist school. Pissarro had insisted that the works of his pupils, Gauguin and Vignon, be included in the 1882 exhibition, and Monet vehemently objected. Monet had also alienated himself from his peers by organizing his own show at *La Vie Moderne* in June 1880. On Renoir's advice he had also submitted work to the Salon: *The Ice-Floes on the River at Bougival* and *Lavacourt*, only the latter of which was accepted. *The Ice-Floes* became the centre of his one-man show, and it was purchased for a relatively large sum of money.

Edgar Degas called him a traitor for denying everything the Impressionists stood for by showing at the Salon, but Monet was perhaps rightly distancing himself from the Impressionist group, who had begun to expand beyond their original precepts into something quite different.

Impressionism had never been a unified school of artists; in fact, their principles and styles were markedly different. The term referred mainly to a popular movement, engaging the talents of a band of gifted

La Promenade, 1875 (detail) (Private Collection). Camille is the model for this work, painted at Argenteuil when Monet was experiencing a flush of prosperity.

Still Life with Apples, 1880 (Chicago Art Institute). Monet painted still-lifes at only a few points in his career – earlier, at a time when he would paint anything for money, and around 1880, when he experimented with a number of floral and fruit displays.

artists who took the unorthodox step of organizing an independent exhibition of their works. Their similarity lay mainly in their shared vision, their community of outlook.

The exhibitions were never restricted to members and not all members exhibited in every one, but problems about who should be allowed to show with the group were beginning to arise. Degas, whose work was more realistic than many of his counterparts' and who consistently shirked the Impressionist label, was keen to encourage new artists. Most of the others in the group saw this as a compromise of the aims and in 1880 Monet's excuse for failing to join the group show was that 'the little clique has become a great club'. He explained his decision, saying, 'I believe that it is in my interest to adopt this position because I can have more confidence in business, in particular with Petit, once I have forced the door of the Salon.'

Monet had a young and very large family to consider; Salon

success was the key to financial stability and he had spent too long seeking this to throw it all away on a movement that appeared to be on its last legs. While he still agreed with its principles, all was well, but there seemed to be a new breed of adherents, some of whom expressed the views of the group in a way that Monet considered wildly unsuitable. It was inappropriate, he felt, to form a coherent ideology for a group that was so divergent, and every attempt seemed to belittle the varied styles of their work. His secession from the group that year was lit upon with glee by the critics, in particular, the paper *Le Gaulois*, who wrote:

> ... *the Impressionist school has the honour of informing you of the sad loss that it recently suffered in the person of Claude Monet ... The burial service for Monet will be celebrated next 1st May – the morning of the opening in the church of the Palace of Industry (i.e., the official Salon) ... please do not attend ...*

Renoir had bowed out of the 1878 exhibition, and Sisley had left the group, doubting the possibility of any future unity and concerned about the increasing use of the Intransigence label. Monet was disillusioned. He was depressed by the enormity of the task involved in keeping his young and adopted families together.

The 1880s would be a decade of restlessness, a period of movement and self-examination; they would lead to some of the greatest paintings the world would ever see.

CHAPTER 3

Lyrical Light

'One day at Varengeville, I saw a little car arriving in a cloud of dust. Monet gets out of it, looks at the sun, and consults his watch: "I'm half an hour late," he says, "I'll come back tomorrow."'

Ambroise Vollard,
En Ecoutant Cézanne,
Degas, Renoir

Overleaf:
The Poppy Field, 1891 (Chicago Art Institute). Monet returned often to the motif of a poppy field in his paintings. *Poppy Field at Argenteuil*, painted in 1873, was much less defined than this later work with its more mature composition.

Vétheuil once again offered Monet the opportunity to paint nature in his own garden. He'd moved most of his favourite potted plants from Argenteuil, and his garden took on an atmosphere of cluttered splendour. His family had always had marvellous gardens; throughout his years with Camille he had travelled often to his aunt's summer house at Saint Adresse, and since then he tried to recreate at every one of his homes a space in which he could work nature to his own devices.

Monet often painted the flowers at Vétheuil. His landlady allowed him to cultivate some land across the road from the house they rented, and he created there an exquisite garden, rich with multi-coloured flowers and plants. The Seine sparkled in the distance, the perfect backdrop for the lustrous foliage. *Flowerbeds at Vétheuil*, in particular, illustrates Monet's mastery of landscape; each flower, each leaf becomes a separate gesture of paint – a flick of the brush, a darting line, a dab here, a dot there. Some of the numerous views that he painted of the village and the countryside were included in the fourth Impressionist exhibition, and his own exhibition in June 1880 had an even greater representation. The growing critical interest in and acclaim for his work would eventually change his fortunes, but for the time being Monet was restless, eagerly seeking new scenes for his work, new countries for inspiration, new colleagues for support, new markets for his paintings.

Monet moved his family with Alice Hoschedé and her children to Poissy, near Paris, in 1881. But Poissy failed to inspire him in any way and they moved again in 1883 to Giverny, on the Seine, where they rented a house. Giverny was a little village in Normandy, quite provincial, and not remarkable in any way but for the garden of the artist who had come to live there. It was a rural village and the occupants were astonished by the Monet entourage of children, which had now expanded to include sons- and daughters-in-law. With some disapproval they uncovered the fact that Alice and Monet were not married and many of the residents greeted the new arrivals with hostility.

It is an amusing vision of Monet which emerged from those early years at Giverny, the irritable older man trailing a menagerie of pets and children, all carrying easels, paints and the increasing number of canvases necessary for him to render a scene. His neighbours must have looked on in horror as he tramped across fields in search of the right scene, the right light. His step-daughter Blanche had already begun to paint beside him, and they were an odd couple, settling themselves in the centre of fields or on the edge of a stream, in order to paint a haystack or a particularly well-lit tree. Ill at ease with their clearly talented but eccentric neighbours, the farmers on adjoining land reputedly charged Monet a toll for crossing their property and it has been

Opposite:
Garden at Vétheuil, 1881 (Washington Art Gallery). Monet's skill as a painter was matched only by his unerring touch in the garden. His garden at Vétheuil, where he moved in 1881 with the Hoschedé family, was a riot of brightly coloured flowers and shrubs, purchased and planted for their ingenious interplay of hues and tones – nature at her finest.

Haystack, Late Summer, 1891 (Chicago Art Institute). One of the *Grainstack* series of paintings, this work was painted in a farmer's field near Giverny; the locals, suspicious of this eccentric painter with questionable moral conduct, took great pleasure in dismantling haystacks as he painted.

said that as he painted they gleefully dismantled grainstacks, changed the angle of their ploughing, or cut down a tree in the middle of his works.

Monet was not a patient man and with his parasol underarm and his sunhat pressed down over his brow, his long, greying beard untidy beneath it, he must have appeared outlandish and unquestionably unapproachable. But as time passed Monet grew comfortable here and he created the home he had so longed for.

From this base Monet travelled a great deal, continuing his relationship with Alice but unable to formalize anything until the death of her husband many years later. Ernest Hoschedé had distanced himself from his family, preferring a bachelor existence in Paris, and he turned his wife and the cost of keeping her and the children over to his one-time friend.

Monet and Alice's relationship was rocky; several letters reveal her intentions to end it – not surprising in light of the fact that he regularly left her with both his and her own children to care for. It would not be long before grandchildren would be part of the household as well, and as Monet's vision for his art grew, he became complacent about the family he left behind on each of his extended painting trips.

But the security of a home was clearly an asset to Monet during this time, for his work showed a new depth and maturity, and he set off on voyages that were increasingly challenging.

He later explained this wanderlust to his friend Thiebault-Sisson:

I felt the need, in order to widen my field of observation and to refresh my vision in front of new sights, to take myself away for a while from the area where I was living, and to make some trips lasting several weeks in Normandy, Brittany and elsewhere. It was the opportunity for relaxation and renewal. I left with no preconceived itinerary, no schedule mapped out in advance. Wherever I found nature inviting, I stopped.

Etretat and Fécamp, also in Normandy, where much of Monet's youth had been spent, were particular favourites, and he struggled to capture their allure in all weathers. He was known to make his journeys most often in the winter months, when he could work undisturbed, and when his own garden was at its least lovely. He adored to witness tormented nature, to document storms, crashing waves, tempestuous winds.

Etretat, the 'French Watering Place' of Henry James, was the subject of much of Monet's work. He is described by locals as braving the autumn storms in even the most shocking conditions: 'Claude Monet, water streaming down under his cape, painting the tempest while spattered with salt water.' He had some near escapes while painting here. In 1885 he wrote to Alice:

Don't alarm yourself ... I was hard at work beneath the cliff, well sheltered from the wind, in the spot which you visited with me; convinced that the tide was drawing out I took no notice of the waves which came and fell a few feet away from me. In short, absorbed as I was, I didn't see a huge wave coming; it threw me against the cliff and I was tossed about in its wake along with all my materials! My immediate thought was that I was done for, as the water dragged me down, but in the end I managed to clamber out on all fours, but Lord, what a state I was in! My boots, my thick stockings and my coat were soaked through. The palette which I had kept a grip on had been knocked over my face and my beard was covered in blue, yellow, etc. ... Anyway I was lucky to escape but how I raged when I found once I'd changed that I couldn't work, and when it dawned on me that the painting ... was done for, I was furious ...

Much of the landscape Monet painted at Etretat was accessible by a steep rocky path, exposed only at low tide. He trudged up and over

Haystack, Thaw, Sunset, 1891 (Chicago Art Institute). Subtly different in mood and atmosphere from each of the others in the *Grainstacks* series, this painting is worked in fresh pastels, the blues receding into the blooming pinks and greens of spring.

cliffs laden with canvases and bags and oil paints, clad in thick woollen clothing and wearing a determined but uninviting expression.

The Etretat paintings were exhibited by Durand-Ruel, but Monet was late in delivering each of them, blaming the weather and the shortness of his visits; there are a large number of his paintings from Etretat which remained unfinished and were sold in a rough state or simply left as part of his estate. He later added some detail to these works, but he was rarely satisfied with his retouching and never convinced that a painting was finished. He said in 1893, 'Anyone who says he has finished a canvas is terribly arrogant.'

Most of his voyages were funded by Durand-Ruel, who was buying Monet again, in response to the sudden demand for the artist's work. There runs between them a lively correspondence over these years – Monet defending his subjects, his schedules and most of all the considerably tardy appearances of his work, and Durand-Ruel fending off constant requests for money.

He regularly spent the advances given to him by Durand-Ruel, apologizing for the work that had not materialized and requesting more funds. His increasing perfection meant that fewer canvases emerged from his clutches, and his growing popularity made them all the more valuable. His excuses were varied: usually the weather was to blame, but occasionally he reminded Durand-Ruel that a painter needed 'peace of mind' in order to produce anything worthwhile, a sly reference to his need for more financial assistance.

From Pourville, on the Channel coast, he wrote to Durand-Ruel:

I can't hold out any longer and am in a state of utter despair. After a few days of good weather, it's raining again and once again I have had to put the studies I started to one side. It's driving me to distraction and the unfortunate thing is that I take it out on my poor paintings. I destroyed a large picture of flowers which I'd just done along with three or four paintings which I not only scraped down but slashed. This is absurd ... Please be kind enough to have some money forwarded to me ...

Monet also painted at Dieppe and Varengeville, both on the Channel, writing home to Alice regularly. His enthusiasm for the fascinating sights he was painting is evident in each of his letters, but so too is the frustration he was obviously feeling. Although it would be incorrect to call it an artistic crisis, Monet was experiencing considerable dissatisfaction with his work and he travelled far and wide, away from his family, in order to rectify the situation.

It was impossible for Alice to accompany him on his trips, and she seems to have resented their frequency and increasing duration. In 1883 he wrote to her from Etretat:

... you need have no fears, I think of you constantly, you can be sure of my love, be brave, I won't be here long. I am working as hard as I can, as I told you yesterday, I am very happy to be here and I hope to come up with something good, in any case I will bring lots of studies back with me so I can work on some big things at home ...

Matin à Etretat, 1883 (Private Collection). Etretat held a fascination for Monet throughout his career and he weathered all of the elements in order to capture its tempestuous beauty.

In 1884, Monet set off for northern Italy, on the edge of the Mediterranean. He travelled alone, concerned that any company would distract him from his task. He wrote to Durand-Ruel shortly before leaving, asking him to keep the visit a secret:

I insist upon doing it alone. Much as I enjoyed making the trip there with Renoir as a tourist, I'd find it hard to work there together. I have always worked better alone and from my own impressions ...

Etretat, The Manneporte, 1885 (Private Collection). Fresh from his trip to Bordighera, in Northern Italy, Monet has invested his palette with deeper, more lustrous colours. Every tiny facet of the rock's façade is indicated by a brushstroke, giving the painting a rich and compelling texture.

If he knew I was about to go, Renoir would doubtless want to join me and that would be equally disastrous for both of us.

At Bordighera, a village just over the Italian border, he discovered a lush and exotic paradise. He stayed far longer than he intended, first struggling to render the colours and dense foliage, and then delighted with his efforts he found it difficult to leave a place of such inspiring landscape. He wrote, 'I climb up, go down again, then climb up once more; between all my studies, as a relaxation I explore every footpath, always curious to see something new.' The light of the Mediterranean fascinated him, and he was excited by the range of colours to which his palette had extended. He wrote to Alice, saying, 'I'm appalled at the colours I'm having to use ... yet I really am understating it.'

Northern France had been best captured with evocative blues and pinks – muted pastels which were light enough to personify the sea mist, the warmth of summer on the air, the fresh sigh of spring in a country meadow. Nature was softened under his brush, becoming a hazy impression. Bordighera represented the opposite extreme of the coast of northern France, where the greys and blues of his most recent paintings created both a sensitive and sensual impression of the character of the air around him. The Mediterranean was, in Monet's words, 'magical', and he painted dozens of canvases during his time here. He used colours like bright orange, turquoise, vivid pinks and aged lemon. He discovered a new emotional outlet in his art, and he struggled to rationalize this with the intrinsic emotions of the location he was painting. Richard Kendall wrote:

> ... *Monet discovered the power of colour to express the higher registers of human experience. Increasingly, he was to discuss his paintings in terms of his feelings and responses to nature, rather than the visual impression made upon him by the scene. Subsequent painting expeditions in the 1880s, such as the trips to Belle-Ile, Antibes and the Creuse valley, were to confirm this departure in this art ... and at Fresslines, beside the River Creuse, he announced, 'I have finally entered into the spirit of this countryside.'*

Following his trip to Bordighera, which yielded over fifty paintings, he spent a month in his studio, reworking the canvases until

Palm Trees at Bordighera, 1884 (Joslyn Art Museum, Omaha). Monet's palette grew to include almost every colour in the spectrum throughout his period on the Mediterranean. He wrote to his wife Alice, 'The palms will make me despair. So much blue in the sea and the sky – it is impossible!'

twenty-six met with his approval and he agreed to sell them. He wrote to Durand-Ruel, that 'I haven't a single canvas which doesn't need to be looked at again, and carefully retouched ... I need to see all my work peacefully, in the right conditions.'

His trip to Belle-Ile produced an equivalent number of canvases and he retired again to his studio to retouch. Interestingly, Monet had always argued that as a landscape painter it was not only necessary but essential for him to work out of doors. He denounced the studio, claiming that only in its natural light could nature be portrayed with any accuracy or feeling. His first insistence upon painting in the open air was established with *Women in the Garden*, painted in 1866 and rejected by the Salon the following year. He insisted that it was 'painted on the spot and from nature, something which wasn't done at the time'. Dr John House is sceptical of Monet's claims:

> ... he seems to have executed few, if any, large paintings out of doors until around 1894. His Salon submissions of the late 1860s show all the signs of being studio compositions, and ... his few large outdoor scenes of the 1870s and 1880s were probably executed in the studio ... However, Monet did undoubtedly work out of doors on his smaller paintings, even in the very severe conditions.

It is clear that while many of his paintings were in fact painted out of doors, his very precise retouching and extremely pedantic finishing techniques were undertaken in his studio, sometimes many years later.

The studio was becoming important to Monet's work. He left Alice for long periods of time, and when he returned he holed himself away to work yet again. He was obsessive about finishing his work, almost always unhappy with the results. He wanted to document the exciting pinks, the fiery reds, the lustrous golds and greens; he found, instead, that he had created another pastel landscape. Today, these paintings sing with energy; then, Monet found them flat.

He returned to the Mediterranean again in 1888, where he stayed at the Côte d'Azure, in the South of France. He was entranced by the contrast of the snowy Esterel mountains, with the raging, resonant blues and greens of the sea. Again, his palette was extended to incorporate new, jewel-like colours. From the Cap d'Antibes, he painted the walled city of Antibes, and his paintings are lustrous evocations of the atmosphere that must have existed – the cool stone thrusting out of the dazzling sea, the creamy mountains presenting a perfectly composed backdrop. He wrote to Gustave Geffroy, a respected art critic and writer, and a friend of Monet's since 1886: It is so beautiful here, so bright, so full of light. One is afloat in blue air. It is awe-inspiring.'

To Alice Hoschedé he wrote:

I am weary, having worked without a break all day; how beautiful it is here, to be sure, but how difficult to paint! I can see what I want to do quite clearly but I'm not there yet. It's so clear and pure in its pinks and blues that the slightest misjudged stroke looks like a smudge of dirt ... I've fourteen canvases underway ...

Monet's new work was successful beyond anything he could have imagined. The lurid colours provoked a reaction among the critics that his pastels had never managed; it was as if the intensity of his palette

View from Cap Martin, 1884 (Chicago Art Institute). In 1884 Monet wrote to Alice Hoschedé, 'I walked to Cap Martin, a famous spot between Menton and Monte Carlo. I saw two motifs there that I want to paint because they are so different from things here, where the sea plays no big part in my studies.'

was directly related to the success of the painting. Surprisingly, Monet was not a content man. He had fought a long battle for a return to financial success and when it arrived he had become entrenched in dissatisfaction with his work. His working practice had becoming increasingly complicated, his use of sometimes a dozen canvases at once made their transportation difficult, and the process by which he moved from one to the other must surely have been cumbersome. He constantly developed his palette to reflect the changing light, but he was less than happy with the result.

He continued to travel over this period, and although his garden at Giverny was beginning to take on the appearance of the haven it would one day become, he was restless and sought new directions for his work. The ever-growing household was a distraction and Monet was surly and disagreeable at the best of times. He suffered from frequent periods of depression, both with his situation and with his art, often failing to complete canvases and occasionally destroying them altogether. In 1890 he wrote to Gustave Geffroy from Giverny:

I'm in a very black mood and profoundly disgusted with painting. It really is a continual torture! Don't expect to see anything new, the little I did manage to do has been destroyed, scraped off or torn up. You've no idea what appalling weather we've had continuously these past two months. When you're trying to convey the weather, the atmosphere and the general mood, it's enough to make you mad with rage.

Monet's depressions deepened, and only a month later he wrote again to Geffroy saying, 'I'm getting so slow at my work, it makes me despair.' His technique had developed by 1890 into something of a comprehensible ideology. He wished, he said to Geffroy, 'to render what I'm looking for: "instaneity" the "envelope" above all, the same light spread over everything'. He began to use long series of canvases together to create the impression of a single subject seen in different lights and atmospheric conditions; he spent months in his studio, reworking, recolouring, away from the light that was his inspiration.

He began to modify the image in front of him in the interest of realizing a more satisfactory colour structure. His experiments with 'instaneity' were the inspiration for his work with a single subject, and he had a portable canvas box which he would use to shift from one canvas to another as the day wore on and the light changed. He said, in 1891, 'For me, a landscape does not exist in its own right, since its appearance changes at every moment; but its surroundings bring it to life – the air and the light, which vary continually ...'

He abandoned all painting but landscapes, restricting himself to paintings in which atmosphere was the prevalent theme. Giverny was

Pink Poplars, 1891 (Private Collection). The *Poplars* series of paintings was painted on the banks of the Epte river, near Giverny. The series was enormously successful, like *Grainstacks*, but Monet deplored breaking up sets for sale.

Nymphéas, 1888 (Toledo Museum of Art). Monet's early paintings of his water garden at Giverny portray the newly planted foliage, shrubs and floral arrangements that would become one of the most beautiful gardens in the world.

becoming a real home for Monet and his family, but he still set out for distant places. He visited his stepson in Norway, where he painted some spectacular snow scenes. He travelled from Christiania and across to Sandviken, writing to Alice daily and offering increasingly weak excuses for his delayed return. *Norway, The Red Houses at Bjornegaard* is a lovely example of his working of snow, which both fascinated and irritated him. He wrote to Alice, 'The place must be infinitely more beautiful without snow, or at least with less than this. The most beautiful feature of the fjords is the water, the sea and it's nowhere to be seen ...'

The turn of the century found Monet in Madrid, London and Venice, and on many of these trips he rode by motorcar. London in particular tempted Monet and he remained there for several months, working from his balcony at the Savoy Hotel and a window of St Thomas's Hospital on the Thames.

His *Thames* series, which includes *The Houses of Parliament in London*, *Waterloo Bridge in the Mist*, *Charing Cross Bridge* and dozens of variations of each of these subjects are the embodiment of his mature talents. The colours are rich and true; purely Impressionist, there is no use of contour or delineations – structures become subsections of his canvas, areas on which to experiment with colour, and at once everything is an impression, a misted image caught in the blink of an eye.

Allow the eyes to glaze over and the colours spill into one another, emphasizing their potency; the composition and the structures

Cliffs near Dieppe, 1897 (Private Collection). Monet travelled less following his marriage to Alice Hoschedé in 1892, but he continued to visit his favourite haunts along the Seine, particularly Dieppe where he had painted in his early days. His maturing technique is evident in the confident blocks of colour.

Waterloo Bridge, Grey Weather, 1900
(Chicago Art Institute). From Monet's
Thames series, which he continued to
retouch for years after its conception on
the banks of London's Thames.

Opposite:
Houses of Parliament, 1900-1 (Chicago
Art Institute). The London weather both
fascinated and enraged Monet, who
returned there three times to paint,
mainly on the Thames.

themselves are immaterial. Their essence, their spirit, their configuration become magnets for a vast array of colours, which are daubed on in tiny brushstrokes to become a remarkable union of air and substance; being and nothingness. The water is dappled with colours from a much brighter palette. Monet had begun to see things differently, to experiment with colours from his travels; emboldened he painted blocks of colour, patterns that changed by the moment, but which he trapped in a splash of intensity on his canvas. 'He was only an eye – but what an eye!' Paul Cézanne said of Monet. Therein lay the intrinsic difficulty which was to plague Monet for the remainder of his life. It was a paradox to make permanent the fleeting, to render in a painting something that existed only in a moment, and in only one man's eye.

Venice offered new and greater challenges. John Singer Sargent, the American expatriate artist and one of the British Impressionists, invited Monet and Alice to spend two weeks in Venice, on the Grand Canal. The Venice of 1908 was a fascinating and cultivated city, punctuated with alleys, tiny winding walks and, most importantly for

Monet, water – canals which passed languorously beside startling architecture. Within a few days he was installed beside them, easels to hand, working through every sunlit hour to capture the changing atmosphere.

The paintings are spectacularly coloured; they have been called 'fairy-like' and 'romantic' and Monet does appear to have succumbed to the idyllic feel of the city. His palette is extraordinarily varied: shades of steamy orange and aquamarine are splashed on to the canvas in *Evening in Venice* and sedate, sensuous blues and greys adopt a silvery, ghostly translucence in works like *Palazzo Contarini*. Yellows and pinks argue in his *Doge's Palace*, emboldened by greens and rich purples to create a symphony of dancing light and colour.

The colours were becoming almost sympathetic with Monet's state of mind. Indeed, Alice was increasingly worried about the

Venice, Palazzo Dario, 1908 (Chicago Art Institute). On his trip to Venice in 1908, Monet wrote to Gustave Geffroy, 'But what a pity that I did not come here when I was younger and more adventurous.'

intensity with which Monet had begun to paint. He became quite fanatical about the hours he worked and although she was able, as the years went by, to accompany him on some of his trips, both of them were growing old and their travels became less adventurous.

Monet had wandered for most of his career, seeking new inspiration in the light, the water, the colour and the atmosphere that he needed as surely as he needed food and water. Following his marriage to Alice, his home became more of a refuge, his garden a paradise. After years of searching, experimenting and investigating, following the path of his artistic development, he had come home to find the world in his garden.

Tulip Field in Holland, 1886 (Musée Marmottan, Paris). Monet visited Holland to paint the tulip fields at the invitation of a prospective patron, Baron d'Estournelles de Constant. Monet's work was becoming increasingly collectable as he sank deeper into a mire of dissatisfaction.

CHAPTER 4

Water Lilies

'The weather is fine, but more Monet than my eyes can bear.'

Edgar Degas

Overleaf:
Nymphéas, 1925 (Private Collection).
Monet's late work was a feast of lurid
reds and oranges; his lily pond had
become an inferno, his Japanese bridge
a bow of flames.

The garden at Giverny was, by 1890, beginning to take on the aspect of a sumptuous haven, brimming with both exotic and common plantlife, elaborately sowed and tumbling with colour and texture. Six gardeners were eventually hired to undertake the upkeep of the garden, one retained specifically to look after the water garden, which Monet built in the early 1890s in a field he had purchased below the house. But the design and the inspiration of what is now one of the world's most famous gardens were clearly Monet's own, for his garden was a carefully woven tapestry, even more eloquently composed than any of his paintings. He dismissed his gardening skills, claiming that he had simply ordered randomly from a catalogue of plants, but the reality betrayed him. He cultivated nature as he had always hoped it would appear. He wrote once from Bordighera, 'I would love to do orange and lemon trees silhouetted against the blue sea, but I cannot find them the way I want them.' What he could not see, what he had travelled the world in search of, he created at Giverny.

The garden was a splendid juxtaposition of colour, lush overgrowth and dense foliage. The hues were harmonized throughout, and as the seasons changed, so did the tones of each overflowing bed. Like his paintings, his garden lacked contours, plants running into one another and falling together in a rush of movement. The garden veritably danced with colour, and it was to fascinate him for the remainder of his life.

Ernest Hoschedé had died in 1892, never recovering, it appears, from the financial troubles which had plagued him. He had turned Alice over to Monet informally, some years earlier, but his death allowed them to make it official, and that they did. By now the Monet household had become over-run with grandchildren, sons- and daughters-in-law, pets, and, as Monet's fame grew, art lovers seeking a glimpse of the famous painter. He had a recognized and determined American following, who set up outside his gate as early as the 1880s; one particularly dogged painter, Theodore Butler, ended up marrying first his step-daughter Suzanne, and then when she died, Monet's other step-daughter Marthe. Monet travelled less after his marriage, finding a deeper comfort in his garden and in the now secure relationship with Alice.

Alice was a warm and welcoming woman, and she took it upon herself to keep Monet's life as free from strife as possible. Their crowded household was run without a murmur, and she ensured that, with their new-found prosperity, they wanted for nothing. After years of hardship, their new comfortable situation was enormously welcome. Always fond of good food, Monet became renowned as a gourmet, hand-writing six books of recipes, and choosing with evident alacrity the meals upon which his family and their very frequent

guests would dine. Although he never cooked, he enjoyed organizing the menus of his ever-growing household, and his taste for luxurious little delicacies was much appreciated. It was a rigidly run household – meals were never late, in the event that Monet might miss an important moment of daylight. Breakfasts were early, and large; lunch always served before noon so that Monet had the best part of the afternoon light in which to paint. They entertained over lunch, rarely in the evenings, for the painter and his wife almost always retired early, in order to be fresh for the morning's work.

These routines became almost sacrosanct, and Monet extremely ill-tempered if they were disturbed. He welcomed guests from around the world, and noted figures of French society and government became regular visitors to Giverny, which was becoming a mecca for art enthusiasts. Many of them set up camp by the walls of the estate,

The Japanese Bridge at Giverny, 1892 (Private Collection). Monet's Japanese Bridge was inspired by pictures of Oriental water gardens he'd studied. It became the focal point for many of his paintings at Giverny.

hoping for a glimpse of, or a titbit of encouragement from, the great artist. Most of them received nothing more than a surly glance as he tramped past, carrying his canvases under an arm or in a wheelbarrow. Monet did not believe in teaching his art, he felt every student must portray his own individual interpretation of what he saw. He was never trained in the academic sense and saw little use in passing on tips that could be misconstrued or, worse, copied.

Inspired by Japanese water gardens, Monet spent a great deal of time and money on his own. Its banks were lined with poppies, agremony, blue sage, dahlias and irises, among others, and bamboos and water lilies were imported to thrust up from its waters. The water garden was originally created to satisfy his need to be near water, and to provide a visual feast which could be enjoyed from a number of outlooks on his property. His pond was fed by the river Ru, and weeping willow and silver birch hung over its edges, caressing the fronds of the greenery and blossoms below. A green wooden footbridge was placed across the pond and it became the central focus of dozens of his works. He said once, 'It took me some time to understand my water lilies. I planted them for pleasure; I cultivated them without thinking of painting them.' But by the middle of the 1890s, they had become a central motif in most of his work.

The water garden became a fascinating point of study for Monet. The reflections of light on the surface of the water, disturbed here and there by the dizzying descent of the dragonflies, the splash of a frog, the movement of an unseen fish became an obsession. The rich expanse of foliage and the deluge of brilliantly coloured and beautifully appointed flowers presented an overwhelming riot of perfectly planned wildness, and exotic growth peeks from beneath the surface of the lustrous pond. He became obsessed with capturing every single effect of light and was often surrounded by a dozen canvases which he quickly rotated as time passed. He gloried in the sunlight; the rain would drive him to angry tears and he would refuse to leave the house. The sunlight created everything his art represented; blackened skies filled him with depression and frustration. He had studios built on his ever-growing property, larger, better lit studios to house the outsize canvases, and the ever-increasing number of paintings in each series.

Rouen Cathedral and the *Thames* in London were early examples of Monet's series paintings. He had become convinced that one painting was unable to do justice to a scene, that a motif must be examined in a series of paintings, which would portray the subtle changes that were, in the end, the makings of a new subject altogether. On his travels from Giverny he was often required to hire a porter to carry his canvases, and a trip abroad would be considered wasted if the weather changed dramatically and he was unable to continue with the work he had begun. The fogs of London had fascinated him, their ever-changing

Rouen Cathedral in the Morning, 1894 (Boston Museum of Art). His paintings at Rouen Cathedral marked the turning point of Monet's serious work with light, in which he undertook to replicate it on a series of canvases. As the light changed he moved from one canvas to the next, capturing the changing effects with broken expanses of colour.

colours swirling and then abruptly changing with the weather. He was exhilarated by London's unpredictable weather – a rare burst of sunshine followed by heavy storms that passed only minutes later, leaving a flush of radiance in the air, fabulous sunsets, sinking in the shrouded mists. But he would be driven to fits of apoplectic anger by the insistent rain which would make it impossible for him to work for days on end. He struggled to paint the atmospheric nuances, returning on three occasions to paint there, determined to create a series which represented the volatility of his subject. He thrust his emotions into his work and they became representations of his infernal energy.

Rouen was another fascination, and the cathedral there enthralled Monet to the extent that he painted no less than thirty representations of its façades, works in which the whole of the front of the splendid building filled his canvas, becoming both the subject and the composition. He painted it as the light changed: he observed the passing effects of light, thoughout the day. For two years, from February to April in each, he recorded the cathedral in various lights and weathers. It became an obsession. He wrote in 1893 to Durand-Ruel, 'I am working as hard as I possibly can, and do not even dream of doing anything except the cathedral. It is an immense task.' The *Rouen* series was

Haystack, 1893 (Springfield Museum). Painted at Giverny, in the fields neighbouring his home, this work represents Monet's spectacular development of colour as light. He painted a series of grainstacks, treating each in a different manner, but always making the stack of grain the central focus of the composition, which some critics found perplexing.

Rouen Cathedral, 1894 (Musée Marmottan, Paris). The paintings at Rouen obsessed Monet, and he returned to paint the same scene many times over two years. There are thirty paintings of the façade of the cathedral in existence, their surfaces so reworked in Monet's quest for perfection that they have been likened to cement.

greeted with enormous critical acclaim; Monet was now considered one of France's greatest painters and buyers came from around the world at the whisper of a Monet sale.

Monet's *Grainstacks* (*Haystacks*) were another tremendous achievement. Formerly Monet's work had consisted of splendid representations of sights seen on his travels. Now he moved closer to home,

Poplars on the River Epte, 1891
(Philadelphia Museum of Art). The
cheerful colours of the *Poplars* series
were one of its main attractions; few
recognized the splendid representation
of changing nature in the works.

working on a single, unassuming everyday sight, which he realized
could be rendered as beautiful and as different by the changing light as
any foreign or exotic subject. *Poplars* was another series, in which the
same visual motif was repeated again and again and studied under the
varying conditions of a day.

Monet's obsessions with single subjects deepened. Always single-
minded he had become fixated. He had been battered day after day by
the elements for most of his working career; he rose early and erupted
at any distraction from his work. His was an explosive personality, one
minute revelling in a gorgeous effect, the next damning the change-
ability of the weather. On one occasion he requested permission from
his local council to remove all the leaves from an oak tree in his garden
when it inconveniently began to sprout greenery. He would not be
cowed by nature. He battled to catch a fleeting effect and stomped off in
a heated temper when he could not. From London he wrote in 1900:

> I've never seen such changeable conditions and I had over 15
> canvases under way, going from one to the other and back again,
> and it was never quite right; a few unfortunate brushstrokes and in
> the end I lost my nerve and in a temper I packed everything away in
> crates with no further desire to look out of the window, knowing full
> well that in this mood I'd only mess things up and all the paintings
> I'd done were awful, and perhaps they are, more than I suppose.

He was dissatisfied with his work. In April of 1912, he wrote to
G. and J. Berheim-Jeune, picture dealers:

> I'm very sorry to inconvenience you, but I find it impossible to
> supply you with any more Venice pictures. It was useless trying to
> persuade my self otherwise, the work that's left is too poor for
> exhibition. Don't insist ... I've enough good sense in me to know
> whether what I'm doing is good or bad, and it's utterly bad, and I
> can't believe that people of taste, if they have any knowledge at all,
> could see any value in it. Things have been dragging on like this for
> far too long ...

At home in his studio Monet would destroy half-finished
canvases and older works, determined that anything with his name on
it should be nothing less than superb. He had seen rough sketches and
paintings of poor quality emerge from Manet's studio following his
death and resolved not to let the same happen to him. But he was
obsessive about his work; good canvases were destroyed in a fit of
pique, whole series slashed and burned on a whim. Eventually age and
the burdensome nature of Monet's work made it necessary to curtail
his trips outside Giverny. A quick change in weather could easily be

Nymphéas, *c.* **1905** (Musée Marmottan, Paris). Monet's water lilies entranced him, becoming a central motif for almost thirty years.

captured, on a canvas stored safely in a studio behind him. It became impractical to carry dozens of canvases and paints with him and Alice's influence no doubt helped to ensure that more and more time was spent at Giverny.

In spite of being a surly fellow at his easel, Monet was popular among his friends, and clearly an excellent host. From his base in Giverny he retained an extremely important position among the artists and writers in Paris, losing many of his Impressionist ties but forging for himself a new status within the intelligentsia. He continued to meet, at the home of another important Impressionist painter, Berthe Morisot, many of his former colleagues, and he attended a monthly dinner at the Café Riche in Paris, to see still others. Of his older friends, Cézanne continued to visit Monet, which both considered an honour – Cézanne because he liked only Renoir and Monet of all contemporary painters, and Monet because Cézanne's work echoed much of what he believed essential to good landscape painting: that nature must be studied at first hand. Cézanne later painted series of landscapes quite like Monet's. Their influence and regard for one another was evident throughout their works. Until his death, Sisley was also a good friend, writing often to Monet and visiting, with the others, the wonderful gardens of Giverny. Their ties weakened when Sisley withdrew from his circle of artist friends, but Monet was instrumental in organizing an auction of paintings following Sisley's death in order to help his children.

The famed French politician Georges Clemenceau also became a great friend and admirer of Monet's, encouraging him in what would be his greatest and final work – an enormous study of the *Water Lilies* entitled *Décorations*, which would eventually appear in The Orangerie at the Louvre. It was a gift to the French state from an artist who had always shunned politics and turned down any honours bestowed upon him from that source, a tribute surely to the remarkable friendship Monet must have shared with Clemenceau.

Renoir remained a friend, and his death in 1919 marked the end of an era for Monet, who had outlived most of his great friends and fellow Impressionists. He had acquaintances in the form of the writers Stéphane Mallarmé and Octave Mirabeau, and the painter Whistler became a close friend. John Singer Sargent was another regular visitor to Giverny.

Nymphéas, 1918-21 (Paris, Musée Marmottan). Monet's brushstrokes grew more confident as he moved closer and closer to the surface of the water; his sky receded out of the painting, the lilies themselves providing the symmetry and horizon.

Monet's family too were a source of joy and increasing support to him as he grew older. They often took turns posing for him in his luxurious gardens, and gamely carried canvases and paints for him as he worked. His letters reflect the warm interest he had in their daily lives, and the great sorrow he felt when one of them left, or worse, passed away. It is likely that the closeness of his extended family kept him sane throughout his many artistic crises, his deep frustrations and enveloping depressions. They encouraged him in his work, created a world for him that was calm and unfettered, allowing him to delight in their day-to-day activities, but keeping from him any unhappiness.

Alice Hoschedé Monet died in 1911 and Monet was crushed by her absence. She had hovered in the background of his life, quietly devoted and always there; he had loved her passionately, and for much of his adult life. She had cared for his children, been nanny, housekeeper, lover and most of all companion and friend. Her death destroyed him and he threw himself even more rigorously into his work. He wrote, 'Nothing in the whole world is of interest to me but my painting and my flowers.' He was attended now by his step-daughter and fellow painter Blanche. Blanche Hoschedé had married his eldest son Jean, bringing the two families into an even deeper union, and she was his constant companion, particularly when Jean was killed in the war, in 1914, leaving her a widow and Monet wild with grief. He wrote to his friend Gustave Geffroy on 10 February 1914, only, 'My poor son died last night,' for once at a loss for words.

But to his garden he retreated, and from those last prolific years come some of the most spectacular and revolutionary paintings of his career. The scope of his work was vast; the canvases enormous, their promise even greater. In 1908, he had written to Geffroy, 'These landscapes of water and reflections have become an obsession. It's quite beyond my powers at my age, and yet I want to succeed in expressing what I feel.' Richard Kendall explains the development of *The Water Lilies*, or *Nymphéas*:

As his obsession deepened, Monet ordered larger canvases and tackled even more audacious confections of colour, tone and texture. Slowly the idea took shape of a unified sequence of paintings, combining the vividness of his perceptions of the lily pond with the ornamental possibilities of its patterns and colours. It appears from the artist's letters that his friend Georges Clemenceau was instrumental in this plan, as it progressed from a modest group of pictures commemorating the end of the War to a large-scale enterprise that required its own building in the centre of Paris.

Nymphéas, 1920-22 (San Francisco Museum of Art). The *Water Lily* paintings required years of painting, overpainting, scraping and retouching before Monet was satisfied with them. Even then, many were discarded and later burnt.

Water Lilies was a tremendous and spectacular climax to Monet's career. The viewer is immersed ever more deeply in the waters and the verdant expanse of the artist's garden, moving closer and closer, where Monet has with his lifetime of acquired technique rendered the light in amazing subtlety, a mosaic of colour in which every nuance, every tiny glimmer is captured and held. The clouds reflect in some paintings, a haze lies languorously over another; the lilies are fresh, elegant, alive. The brushwork has been set free, daubing, swirling, escaping the rigid lines of his earlier work to swoop through the light, capturing a reflection here, a current there, a breath of air that has stirred a frond of eelgrass. Morning, evening, midday were captured, as was every consecutive moment that joined them, the colours of his palette changing subtly as the light shifted, as a cloud stole over the sky, as a wind picked up the surface of his pond. The water lilies are perfectly composed, never boring, never the same. The series is breathtaking.

Monet's technique was described by Kendall, who noted:

> ... *[his technique] shows a number of bold departures from his earlier work, as he built up crusts of multicoloured pigment and gestured with his brush on a scale unthinkable a decade earlier ... Working with a large brush Monet would introduce the dominant colours of the motif while drawing in the principal forms of the composition. A number of highly simplified sketchbook drawings from this period show the importance the artist attached to these underlying rhythms, using them to animate and unify ... Dense pitted areas of overpainted brushwork were set against thinner and more delicate passages of colour, deep shadows contrasting with shimmering, sensuous highlights.*

Huge canvases were joined side by side to create the decorative effect he sought, but portraying at the same time the movement through the day at the pond – an exploration of the moods and emotions of the setting; a celebration of light, atmosphere, everything he had spent his whole life struggling to arrest. He constantly retouched, rarely happy with a finished work, but eventually he began to hand them over to Clemenceau, who fought on behalf of the painter to have a circular gallery specially constructed for them. In the end they were hung in two oval rooms at the Orangerie, in what the painter André Masson called 'the Sistine Chapel of Impressionism'.

From 1908 Monet's eyesight began to fail and shortly afterwards he was diagnosed as having cataracts. He had once, as a young painter, wished to be blind, suddenly to be allowed to see, not knowing what anything was, not knowing any names, just able to paint something as he saw it. As his vision dimmed, it looked as if he might get that wish. Despair overtook him, and the growing formlessness of his work throughout this period is attributed to his failing sight. Clemenceau, managed to convince Monet to undergo surgery to remove the cataracts, and the artist reluctantly agreed. Miraculously, his sight was restored, and he continued to paint until the last months of his life, the fire in his soul venting itself on richer, more wildly vibrant colours, rushes and swirls of the paintbrush that turned his garden into a blaze of glorious reds, vermilions, burnished oranges and brilliant greens.

Even as his health failed, Monet struggled to work. He wrote, in September 1926, to Georges Clemenceau, '... I was thinking of preparing my palette and brushes to resume work, but relapses and further bouts of pain prevented it. I'm not giving up that hope and am occupying myself with some major alterations in my studios and plans to perfect the garden. All this to show you that, with courage, I'm getting the upper hand.'

His work attracted attention around the world; he was at last wealthy and famous, but aside from the comfort it accorded his lifestyle, he despised the distraction. He was the greatest exponent of Impressionism; his later work was the precursor for abstractism and for much of modern art. Today, his paintings are as highly regarded as those of any other pioneer of art. He painted in his garden, usually a solitary figure, the supreme master of Impressionism capturing over and over again the impressions cast upon his mature eyes, rendered heroically by his seasoned talents, made almost surreal with the provocative palette of his final days.

Monet died in December 1926, at the age of eighty-six. He had said, once, 'I would like to paint as the bird sings'; his power to endure, to delight so naturally, has made his words prophecy.

Irises by the Pond, 1919-25 (Chicago Art Institute). Monet planted the flowers in his garden at Giverny in order to have something to paint when the weather was bad. In the end, the garden became one with his art.

INDEX

Monet. Camille, 1866
(Bremen Kunsthalle)

Monet: Women in a Garden, 1866-7
(Musée d'Orsay, Paris)

Monet. Boulevard des Capucines, 1873
(Nelson-Atkins Museum of Art, Kansas City)

Monet. Garden at Vétheuil, 1881
(Washington Art Gallery)

Monet. Pink Poplars, 1891
(Private Collection)

Monet. Houses of Parliament, 1900–1
(Chicago Art Institute)

Monet. Rouen Cathedral in the Morning, 1894
(Boston Museum of Art)

Monet. Nymphéas, 1920-22
(San Francisco Museum of Art)